Pieces of the Soul

Amy N. Turner

authorHOUSE®

AuthorHouse™
1663 Liberty Drive
Bloomington, IN 47403
www.authorhouse.com
Phone: 1-800-839-8640

First published by AuthorHouse 9/28/2009

ISBN: 978-1-4389-8954-9 (e)
ISBN: 978-1-4389-8952-5 (sc)
ISBN: 978-1-4389-8953-2 (hc)

Library of Congress Control Number: 2009909041

Printed in the United States of America
Bloomington, Indiana

This book is printed on acid-free paper.

There are some folks without whom this couldn't have happened. So here's your spotlight:

Debbie, for always encouraging me to write and being willing to proof my 3 am typos and word confusions. The reason this all looks so great is because of her mad English teacher skills. I can't tell you how much it means to me that you were willing to do this.

Giana (Mama Duck) and J Sunny, for activating those fantastic Virgo twin powers of yours and helping me start to get everything in order. There is flow because of these awesome ladies. Two of cups!

J2B, for helping me to finally have an about the book and about the author. Thank the Divine he stepped in and saved the day on that.

My sisters (Rizzie, Nikki, Lana, and Taz) have been incredible for putting up with my spaztasticness (I did, in fact, just make that word up. They are used to that.) during this process. Love you.

Mom and Dad, for being you (so that I could be me) and for never having any doubt that I could pull this off.

Sam, my High Priestess and friend, for dubbing me Priestess of Words, which reminded me where one of my core talents lies, and for demanding an autographed copy before I'd even signed the contract. Your faith in me has been incredible and much appreciated. Two of cups and blessed be.

For Mom –

couldn't have done it
wouldn't be me
my views would be so different
my world not the same

if not for you.

Thanks.

Light of Your Life

A NOTE TO THE READER:

Welcome, welcome, to the realm of my soul and my imagination. I feel that I should warn you that not all that follows is light and unicorns and rainbows. Not all that follows is about love and happiness. The contents are my ups and downs, but also my attempts to understand the world around me. My inspiration comes not only from my own emotions (although there is a lot of that) but from my empathy and sympathy for others. There is anger and bitterness and darkness in some of the pages ahead. Just so we're clear: there is grit and beauty and sometimes they coexist.

This project began as an attempt to create a unique gift for my mother, someone who has always been an inspiration for me. She has been both my mother and my friend for my whole life and I consider myself lucky for that. Somewhere along the road, it took on a life of its own and here we are – a real, published and available to the whole world, book. Quite the process, but in the end, it's still a unique gift for my mother. You just get to see it, too.

Enjoy yourself.

> "...And I feel like I'm naked in front of the crowd
> Cause these words are my diary screaming out loud
> And I know that you'll use them however you want to..."
> ~ "Breathe (2 AM)" by Anna Nalick

TABLE OF CONTENTS

FICKLE

sometimes
stumbling, clumsy
the words come slowly
grudgingly, reluctantly

sometimes
rushing, tumbling
the words come quickly
lustily, heartily

sometimes
thoughtfully, wonderfully
the words create art
beautiful, powerful

just sometimes

CRADLED PROMISES

the light of dawn
- pink and pale -
dancing over the barren trees
its cool fingers
reaching towards the
awakening world

the misting rain
- light and fine -
tickles the skin
and whispers at
the face, the hands

waiting for the others,
the quiet of the night dissipating
the sounds of the
rising sun stretching
washing over the ears
and the soul

promises of a new beginning
cradled in the hands
of the infant day

BLANKETED IN STILLNESS

never is the world
more quiet,
still,
than in the early hours
of morning after
snow
has fallen

when the darkness
of night is
fading
and the world,
blanketed
in white,
is soft, soothing

the cold, crispness
of the morning air
momentarily
stuns
before wrapping
you in its
embrace

staring out the
window at the
quiet
of the world
reveling in its
stillness,

the softness of the sky,
and the dusting
of white
clinging to everything

not even the sound
of cars
really shatters the
stillness

AURORA

hushed
the silent dawn stretches
itself above the horizon

the black of night
shifting to a hazy
blur of hues

black into blue
into purple
into reds and oranges

still and awed
driving home
at twilight

as the first rays of
the morning caress
the treetops

MIGRAINE

pounding
eyes ache, sharp stabs
as the sun rises
throbbing
bile rising, burning deep
an explosion at the temples
pain rolling in waves
crashing through me
time the enemy
- so long until the darkened safety
    of my bedroom -
strength of will keeping me going
.... driving.... stamina waning

until i am within my safe haven
and succumb to the bliss of sleep,
the great healer

CHERRY BLOSSOMS

blanket of
soft white purity
brushing the skin as it falls
covering the ground
gentle breeze carrying the
lightest of fragrances
across the way
walking, catching
the blossoms in hair, on the sleeve
silky soft against fingertips
fragile beauty
dramatic against the blue
of the sky

SIMPLICITY

there is simplicity
in being plain
there are no high expectations
no repeat performances of
impossible beauty

instead of the surface,
others see my wit,
my intelligence, my compassion
instead of a pedestal,
others honor who i am
on the ground

still, there was an envy
of beauty in others
(slim of build, fair of hair)
of beauty (outward) i did
not see in me

until now

UNTITLED

i marvel sometimes
at the conflict within
the eternal desire to be
what i'm not
and the nonexistent motivation
to force the change

my heart wishes something from myself
it yearns for change, for a difference
to be noticed, to be seen

my mind laughs at the heart's folly
seeing the truth, knowing reality
invisible, unnoticed,
unwanted

i see others around me
happy, laughing, joyous
even in the moments of anger
there is still an iridescence,
shimmering and delicate,
a peace in unity

i wish for it
hope, dream of it
and know its not meant to be

HORIZONS

there's a small
place inside
where the joy
at your love and
happiness is oh so gently
tempered
- not tarnished or broken -
just softened
smoothed over
quieted
ever so slightly

there's a tiny spark,
barely noticeable,
of jealousy
not directed at you

but more at the
loneliness within
because i don't
have that
and it leaves me
wondering
if i will

still, despite this
inner disquiet,
i celebrate with you
(because you deserve
this happiness)
all while glancing to
the horizon

MIRROR MIRROR

mirror mirror
on the wall...

who is she, looking
back into my eyes?
she's watching me
apprehension and puzzlement
written across her face

what does she think of me
i wonder
as i stare back at her
trying to figure out from
whence she came

i can't remember when
i first realized she was there
instead of who i thought
would be looking back

what do we do when
the futures we imagine
are gone
no warning, just...
gone?

who is she, looking
back into my eyes?
she has my face...
or does she?

LOST

stumbling
i walk through a maze
of mixed messages
and clouded signals

uneasy
i trip over my own inexperience
my secret fears and
confusion seeping in

there are no maps
no signposts or guides
i've lost my way
alone and sad

waiting
i hold my breath
searching for hope,
for joy or even contentment
but in vain

UNTITLED

words
jumbled and confused
dancing through my mind
as i try to
understand

thoughts
wild and racing
struggling to rein them in
as i try to
explain

feelings
fleeting and ephemeral
wisps that i cannot grasp
as i try to
say

where i am
who i am
this very moment

FALLING APART

falling apart
pieces scattering
in the deep dark
crouched and hiding

tear-streaked face
my soul withering
reaching out to the
nothingness around me

feeling so lost
tumbling down
never ending crevasse
swallows me whole

hollow and cold
wandering long
shadowed lanes
of half spent wishes

falling apart
pieces scattering
in the deep dark
crouched and hiding

DROWNING

one drop

one drop
and I am drowning

in unrepentant believers
in an unachievable dream

whose path leads through
a forest of abandoned mysteries
and unwanted answers

one drop

and I am submerged
surrounded by translucent fantasies

where eternity is now
and memory is tangible

one drop

one drop
and I am drowning

VEHEMENCE

there are days
i just want to roll back over
submerge into fantasy
forgetting the banality
of day to day existence

my life isn't horror
it's not even all that interesting
most days

it's the scary little dark part
deep in me
that i wish to avoid
that makes me huddle
small and childlike
the mask, the defense,
the armor that kept me safe
through the early years
the tumultuous years

the fiery, raging fury
which swept over all
and left naught in its wake -
not even ashes -
for it was so hot and bright

that sword, still sharp,
still gleaming bright
has been sheathed.
i have little need for
it now

from time to time
it comes, unbidden,
a habit, an addiction
a double edged sword that
scars us both, victim and me

it's part of me

but it frightens me all the same

FRUSTRATION

the brush of skin
fingertips on the wrist
unassuming
innocent
filled with a suppressed longing
and an echoing loneliness

a glance
eyes bright with humor
and curiosity
wondering about the
innuendo, subtle but present

signals dancing
flickering like dying firelight
on a crisp winter night
hard to follow
impossible to catch

adrift in a sea
of emotion
no compass to guide me

i don't know what to do

LONELINESS

it is not old age
that gives me chills,
leaves me shivering and frightened
nor death
(though i cannot deny it leaves me
unsettled and uncomfortable)
and its dark embrace -
it is a more subtle, grayer thing
a shadow of a fear
that is weighty and suffocating
once it has filled your soul
you become hollow
a ghost
haunting, enduring
once that darkness has
seeped in through the cracks
cold tendrils creeping around you
the chill of it
makes the passage of time
unending
it is hard to allow yourself
hope
in love

UNTITLED

what do you do when faith
abandons you to a
quiet solitude?
how do you regain what
is lost
in a slippery moment?
the inner strength that
   surprises when it arrives -
how do I get that? from where?
how do I know it will come for me?
when others look to me for
   reassurance....
who gives it to me?
drifting, lost, confused
no answers forthcoming

UNTITLED

the roots of my
struggles reach deep
into my core,
making change a
heart-wrenching process
letting go of old habits and
beliefs
(unhealthy but familiar and safe)
the road that i've
chosen is long
and
i've seen many potential
me's ahead
though nothing is set in stone
(and the pain of the change is great)
the lit match is in my hand -

i'm ready to let it go

UNTITLED

just thinking about
the process
– take a deep breath –
my heart rate starts to dance
   á la Riverdance
– close your eyes and count to ten –
my stomach welcomes in a hurricane,
   complete with a roiling sea
– imagine your favorite place –
my head could float away, a
   balloon controlled by the slightest breeze
and yet...
i feel like i'm glowing with joy
i can't wait to get started

another year passed
new faces, familiar faces
accommodating and adapting
to new thoughts and reactions
working through conflicts and
    miscommunications (just within)
coming together to manage
    crisis after crisis
teasing and joking, laughter
    building the connection
surviving the shut down
    and coping with the changes
    at reopening
reintegrating into familiar (and
    unfamiliar) patterns
gearing up for another year

UNTITLED

stressful. harried. chaotic.
typical descriptors of a typical day
can't make this stuff up.
also apropos to our setting.
a unique blend of personalities,
   fluid from day to day.
that's us.
days of frustration also are filled with
   laughter.
days of running non-stop also are filled
   with moments of support and generosity.
despite all those dark moments,
   it is the humor, the kindness,
   the friendships and generosity
that bring us back each day.
it is the difference we make
   individually and collectively
that helps us walk in the door

UNTITLED

no trust?
really?
probably the best and largest team
managing crisis after crisis as a team,
   without forethought,
there has to be *some* trust.
otherwise, nothing would ever get done.
no one would ever go home if there was no trust.
maybe, now blind to what trust exists
   because of frustration and disappointment,
you've lost the ability to see what's here.
and maybe trust levels aren't as high
   as they could be.
but it's there.
   we can build on it.
if you're willing to take a leap of faith.

fascinating
the descent into
madness

reality that
simultaneously
is what you see
and nothing like it

who is real
what is real

indistinguishable

the real question is
which of us is mad -
the one who sees
        or
the one who doesn't

attention
   now

seeking, grasping
grip tight, steel

say anything
just stay a moment longer
talk with me

needing
a moment
a reassurance
a direction

needing
anything, everything

pulling it all
within myself
filling the dark void
the emptiness

hollow and blank

taking from others
what
i
don't
have

some highs can't be recreated
they're extraordinary in how
    far they take you
out of the despair, the poverty, the
    ennui of monotony
they fill you to overflowing
    - vibrant, rich, exotic -

but they're a bitch, too

they drop you lower than you ever
    believed that you'd be
lethargic, listless...
uncaring and devoid of anything

goddamn

and so the chase begins to
    have it all again
- no one told you that you'd only
    really get it once -

how far can you run? how long?
before it all gives way
to
nothing

what horror, twisted and sharp
blurs that ever so fine line
what determines the distinction
between real sensory experience
  and hallucination

fear, gnawing and strong,
grins wolfishly at those
who cannot distinguish
the voices of friends real
and enemies imaginary
so that friend and foe coexist
in the same shattered reality

worse still, to be trapped
in a belief system, skewed so
far to one side that it is close
to coming crashing down

and the only solution
a complex web of interactions
- a rainbow of tablets -
that dull the beauty of the world
(quash the spirit and
shackle the soul)

a small percentage of
the world cursed so
a barely larger percentage
who see, who understand and
who reach out willingly

the rest? they shun
afraid of the taint
and laughing cruelly
at the incoherent stream
of syllables uttered
by the afflicted

how can this
be reality?

ADDICTION

feel it burning
deep inside
- liquid fire -
on a precipice,
teetering dangerously
the longing a sharp
pain ripping you apart
the bitter taste at the back
of the throat
- can't keep anything down -
trembling
wanting
needing
so strongly you shatter into
millions of jagged pieces
that you barter away
to ease, smooth, dull
the addiction

UNTITLED

systemic despair
the agony of stagnation
overextension
of resources
of people
to meet
the tidal wave of
needs
not enough
  money
  support
  understanding

what now?

30 DAYS

hands trembling, knees giving out
the tears start running down my face

30 days. 1 month.
it's not nearly enough time.

energy slowing, body losing
the fight
against the invasion

wanting to help you,
spare you from the pain
but not wanting to let go
not yet

30 days.
how do you say goodbye to a part of you
in just 30 days?

FORGIVENESS

i wish

i wish that i could
only remember
what was happy
about you

the many, many
silly things you did
your love and affection
for us, unalterable

i wish

i wish that i could
forget the horror
and the sorrow
from the 30 days

that were really
less than 10
blur away how
you looked at me

in the cold, clinical
office, sad and a little
scared, trying to get
away by climbing in my lap

as i held your head
in my lap and
let them put you
to sleep
stop your heart
stop the illness

that moment
etched brightly
brilliantly
in my mind

is what haunts me
still

in my heart i know
i have your forgiveness

i just wish

i had mine

1 YEAR

the heavy ache
deep
in the darkest, quietest places
of my soul

untouched by
the brine caking my face
unrelieved by
my ragged breaths

so heavy
i can hold it out to you
its dark opaque surface
without reflection
taking everything in:
pain, sorrow, grief, guilt

i awoke
my head thick
my body slow
quiet and hollow

a teardrop stained on a wooden box
as a monument to a year of recovery
mingled with regret

HEARTACHE

sharp and deep
the breath i take
at the first sound of tears

that moment of fear
of horror
that someone caused this

that someone hurt you

the rage, the inherent
desire to fix it, to
protect my kin, my kith

my soul

a razor-edge, biting into
the fabric of my soul
as your pain pours into me

swallowing it up
to spare you, to save you

i'd take it all in
(if i could)

to give you a
small moment

of peace

it is the people we trust most
our blood, bones, and soul
the length of time within us
that we fear most

their power is in everything
their love, despair, and status
within our personal microcosm
of the world
and it is always the subtle
the sly remark
the offhand comment
the whisper, the glance
the lack of touch
- physical or emotional -
that strikes the very core

everyone is wounded

our wounds run deep
they are our medals
from a battle that raged in
a field of betrayal
that can't ever be left behind

we are
the somnambulists of our era
walking, wounded veterans
who forgot how to be children

the future cannot
erase the injuries
of the past
ease them, maybe, if one is lucky enough

there is no bandage to cover the hurt that
reaches inside the soul

so we walk on, wounded,
and hope to find better through
the choices we make

FOR DAWN

Gone into the Lord's embrace
Lady's gentle touch full of grace
The path to Summerland bright and clear
Our memories of you we'll hold dear
Lessons taught and example set
Know that you were merrily met
Our sorrow will ease as time goes by
Our smiles return, our tears will dry
A peaceful rest you've more than earned
As the Wheel continues to turn
Our goodbyes we now will say
Until we meet again one day

FADED GREY

ash clings
to my fingers
as i let go, a tiny
bit, of you

my fingers now
shaded grey
a grey i never
want rinsed off

but the salt water
i wiped from my
cheeks has all
but erased it

not you, though,
even empty, i
cling to you,
to memory

hoping the
hollowness
fades, but that
you, stay

MAMAW

the light is always so pretty
filtered through stained-glass
(the powder blue coffin, so cold)

it dances across the pale
faces, so the tears become rainbows
(so many flowers, bright, death colors)

it softens the harsh look they
tried to hide with rouge and lip color
(you never looked like that in life)

it rests gently around the shoulders
of my cousin, who tries not to cry
(you wouldn't have liked such a fuss)

the dancing soft light reminds me
of you, when you smiled at me
(i miss you)

JIM

to me, you
were the granddaddy i never knew
somehow i know
he would have been a lot like you

he would have been
funny and strong and smart
he would have had a presence
that was laughter and love

he would always
ask me how i was
how was school going
and care about the answer

to me, you
were the granddaddy i never knew
somehow i know
he would have been a lot like you

GRIEF

pain
trickling
through my body
cold and sharp
trickling
into my heart
freezing and breaking
trickling
down my salty cheeks
tasted bitterness

the days have rolled by
the tears have stopped falling
(mostly) when i say
your name
telling others about you
with laughter, in love
sharing that joy you
brought to my life
has eased the jagged
pain in my heart
now, a dull ache,
that just rests within
nestled in my love
that i will always have
for you

GAIA

warm, little
affection from the beginning
(cold, wet nose and all)
sitting in my lap
chasing my fingers

tripping, herding
walking between our legs
(should have named you underfoot)
looking up
loving

warm, big
breathing isn't easy
(i had to hold you in my arms)
sleeping
at peace

goodbye

4 YEARS

time passed –
  4 years –
now back in your home
(i remember that first day...
   unpacking the box
   giving you a new space
   in this familiar abode)
how strange to be here
  without you
sometimes i hear you
  scrambling 'round the corner to greet me
sometimes i see you
  sitting at the top of the stairs, head cocked
it's these moments
  – bittersweet –
when the grief rears its head
and my soul aches

TEN YEARS

ten years of memories
laughing at your silly antics
scolding you for causing mischief
waking up to your excited bark
- or worse, your cold nose against
my skin, ick -
we brought you home and
you were so tiny, so curious
you stopped being tiny but
remained nosy, always
i cannot eat ice, cucumber
without thinking of you
pawing, begging, watching intently
the warmth of you, your fur
against me on the sofa
while you snoozed, content
just a few memories from
ten years of love

SAMHAIN

i awake
in the golden glow of
early afternoon
– not quite time to get up –
curled next to me
a bundle, wrapped up
in itself
– it stirs –
sleepily, stretching
paws forward
purring
before resettling against
my side
silky and soft
we fall back asleep
together

GRANDPA

why did you think it was ok?
i was struggling
gasping
begging for air
i pushed and pushed
hoping the sweet air would come
i was afraid
terror building, building
suffocating
and there she was
making you stop

why did you think it was ok?
all i wanted to do was talk
waiting
patiently and anxiously
hoping
you talked to daddy
but not to me
although i was the reason we called
and you kept talking to him
but making excuses not to talk to me
so he hung up

it's okay now
i have made my family
it's made up of blood
and not blood
friends and relatives
but not you
you are not family
you are just genetics
and i don't need you anymore

tightness
in my jaw,
shoulders...

sharp intake
of breath -
waiting...

the gilded
words -
dulled by their
insincerity -
fall from
your lips

ashes from
a cigarette,
potent and cloying

wishing you
away
or quiet

to bask in
the silence
of
truth

DOUBT

i stand in your shadow
uncertain, hesitant
i know better than to
trust myself, my abilities

time and again
you taught me that
not fast enough, good
enough, smart enough

i learned
(like thomas)
how to doubt, to
scrutinize every small
moment
from you

now, i turn from the
accolades, the laurels,
ducking my head
ashamed, embarrassed

knowing that they
cannot be for me

REPETITION

quiet and insidious
fingers slowly wrapping around
unnoticed, invisible
the tightness surprising
unexpected

a languid smile
pleased with itself for
its stealthy approach
cleverly disguised -
a new cloak over a
familiar face -

immobile within its clutch
this fear of the past
in a wholly new circumstance

afraid of the past repeating
with someone else

2 AM

2 am
and we're still on the phone
hard to believe there was
a time that we didn't talk much
didn't poke or
check in

not many friends still awake
least of all working and capable
of talking at length
about foolish
things

lucky there are still friends
who can keep me
laughing and on
my toes

KINDRED

Strangers whose eyes met
oh, so briefly - and,
while I do not know you,
I feel like I understand.
In the glint of your eyes, knowing,
and the warmth of your smile,
I saw a kindred soul.
Your words - both captivating and
exquisite -
I've found the essence of them
in my own craft, my own thoughts.
Were our worlds to overlap,
the irrevocable change,
what then?
Deep within, in the very quiet part of my soul,
a small piece of me longs to know.

THE OTHER NIGHT, I DREAMT...

the other night, i dreamt of wide blue skies
and rolling hills dancing with wildflowers

when the storm came
i thought of you, your energy

the first bolt of lightning knocked me
off my feet and as i fell
the dark clouds rolled over me,
cushioning my fall

enveloped by the swirling energy
chaotic, powerful
i thought it would wholly overwhelm me
until the first ray of light filtered through

warming my skin
i was free to stand on my feet again
and was startled to realize

i already was –

UNTITLED

i could see you
sneaking up behind me while i'm playing with art
slipping your arms around me and laughing while
i smear just a little bit of the pastel
on your hand, on your face

i could see us
warm in an embrace
blues and reds and greens soft
across our skin as i trace the
curves of you

i could see you,
back turned, your ghosts tugging on
your sleeve, your soul
struggling to let go of the past
and losing today

CHIMERA

awed, i watched as you
walked into my dream
very real, very warm
you reached out to me,
took my hand, and
we started walking

the sun filtered through the leaves
and the golden green glow
settled around us, soft and
reassuring
it hugged us gently as we walked,
you and i

our discourse ranged from
the very smallest pieces
of our lives to the
overshadowing events of the world
it was then that i felt it

the bridge between our souls

my heart, weighted by your
imminent departure, hoped for more
but, alas, you kissed my hand
and turned away

you walked slowly into the distance
and as the dream faded
i heard the whisper of a voice,
powerful and sage, say
that we would find each other

our eyes would be the key

DY

i wonder about you
how has life been, has
it treated you well

i wonder
are you well
are your dreams all coming true
what's it like having your heart's desire

i think of the past
without regret, without anger
you have a place there
you always will

there's no room for you now
that gaping hole you created
in your hurry to break away
in your desperation to create a
new image of you

it's healed now
filled by new experiences
filled by new people
who value me and all that i am

thank you for giving me the chance
to find these people
for allowing me the room i needed
to fit them into my life

we've gone our separate ways
different paths, different directions
what surprises me is that still,
despite everything else,
we give each other gifts

UNTITLED

churning, knotting
twisting in on itself

my stomach roils
and plummets

senses heightened
hands shaking
palms sweaty

the urge to just
tell you everything

all the little secrets
all the dark places
scratched and grimy

pull them into the light
so you can see

that little thrill of fear
caught in the back of my throat
the panic gripping me
that you will turn away

keeping it covered,
buried deep
shying away from discovery

safe

TRICKS OF THE LIGHT

tricks
of the light
keep me from seeing the truth

the truth of
you -
and of me -

illusion, to think
things will remain
how you want

tricks
of the light
keep me from seeing the truth

in your eyes
obscured by dusk and deceit
is the coldness i never imagined
lives in you

in my heart
fooled by hope and memory
is the wound i never imagined
you would inflict

tricks
of the light
keep me from seeing the truth

i was blind

UNTITLED

bitterness, hard choices,
disinterest and
forgetfulness, these
are your gifts to those you
left behind

reaching out
shaky, hurt
i thought, for me,
you would return

once a bond so strong
kept us together
a power, a hum that
created a connection i
thought would never break

not even for me -
for my salty tears
or my broken heart -
did you look back

UNTITLED

your reflection
rippling in the water
slippery and ethereal
like your presence
in my life

the photograph
a corner folded, worn
thin and faded
like my memories
of you

all there is is past
no future, no horizon
we have nothing
to look forward
to because it's
gone

PIECES

in one fell swoop
you crushed my world
everything i knew crumbled
what was truth is now a lie

in one moment
you sent my world spinning
careening into the mists
lost in the vast darkness

in just a few little words
you broke my heart
ripped apart my soul
and destroyed my faith
in you

YOU, ME, AND THE END

i don't
remember
the beginning,

you, me and the end

there was
laughter, happiness
sharing, smiles
even with
space

which grew
wide and deep
and then,
(when, I'm not
sure)
change
subtle but building,

rolling black clouds
blotting out the sunshine of us

i don't
remember
the beginning,

you, me and the end

but here we are

UNTITLED

faith in you
cost me

i look around
people i care for
i once trusted
now unsure

trust in you
cost me

months of
wondering
is it safe
frightened

not hate but
resentment
fills me

it is not a
payment i
was willing
to make

UNTITLED

faith and trust
so paper thin, stretched taut
so fragile - the gentlest touch shreds -
though once strong and vibrant

my thoughts troubled
confused and dark
not comprehending
the stranger with the familiar face

we're at a point
looking over the edge
into the shadowed depths
the choice to build
or to let go
before us

emotions overlapping
overriding one another
one moment angry, the next
complacent, indifferent

so uncertain, so unsure
no direction or idea
lost within a once familiar landscape
the rules have been erased
without warning

where do we go from here?
there is no way back,
that bridge is gone
you set fire to it and it burned
brilliantly

what is it you want of me?
I have given all I can and more
I'm empty, drained
you took all there was
without a second's thought

seeing your face
once brought reassurance,
warmth, friendship
now it brings naught
but hurt, doubts, and pain

how could you do this?

SOLITUDE

it's not as though i
am incapable of squeezing
- breath held -
between the immovable rock
of who you are
and the cold, rigid, and steely
hardness of circumstance

wily and possessed of an
unnamable spirit, i could
dance between the two points
- bare breaths apart -
like leaping over a bonfire
roaring on a late winter's night

luring you in, pulling you
under the spell of my desire
my song, sweet and velvety,
entrancing you slyly
making you mine

that power is within me
i feel it, sense it
fluttering, weightless
a ripple across the surface
of my heart

but i'm lost, without a
guide
no one to show me
how to harness the
fiery power within

and i'm left, the shadow
of you just out of reach,
somber and in solitude

PATRIOT

can you be born a patriot?
my mother was

inherent were the notions of
duty, valor, honor, pride
her service was not
out of obligation,
rather a privilege that she
masterfully transformed
into a career

can you be born a patriot?
i was

growing up i watched
her dress in the blue uniform
pride filling me with each step
the name tag
the shoulder boards
the tie tab

laughing at the old taunts
because she did wear
combat boots
- when wearing BDUs -
not much of an insult, really

how can you not be one

seeing the daily struggles
- a woman in command -
raising a strong-willed daughter
(having learned that from
    my idol)

knowing that she had
chem warfare gear in the car
(just in case)
and drove different routes
to work
(so no one could follow)

there's no other end product,
other than patriot.

mock, scoff, do as you will -
30 years of her life
(and 18 of mine)
afforded you that luxury.

MY STUDY

you are my study
in love
you are my model
through your
grace
compassion
generosity
warm smile
i have learned how
to interact with the world
i have learned to face my fear of rejection
i overcame it - well, most days, anyway -
i have the strength within
(you taught me how to use it)
now, if only i can find
someone with whom i could share
my knowledge of love

UNTITLED

lost
dizzy with the rush
fingers tingling
heart pounding
eyes alight
- amazement flooding -
breath coming fast
licking lips
reaching out tentatively
- such beauty -
wanting to feel, to know
truth

UNTITLED

paint dripping from my fingertips
kisses raining from your lips
charcoal smeared on my cheek
heat of your body next to mine
glitter in my hair
tangled in your fingers
watercolors stain my skin
you leave an impression on my pillow
i've drawn our love as best i can
in your arms

i heard your spirit on the wind
soft, gentle, scared...
i felt your heart in the sun glinting in my hair..
warm, delicious, smooth...
when rain fell I tasted your tears,
bitter, angry, frightened...
when the wolf growled and bared his teeth, i did not fear -
because i saw your insecurity -
and i opened my arms

LAST NIGHT

i dreamed of you last night
you smiled at me and i melted
into eternity

your words filled me like endless light
blazing forth from your soul
brilliant blinding
warm

you opened your world
and i wanted to fall in
just fall and never land
weightless and free

you held out your hand
and i reached
fingertips brushing
sending energy pulsing through my skin

when i woke up you were gone
the morning cold and gray
emptiness and sadness beckoning
then i remembered
fluttering and hopeful

i dreamed of you last night

HANDS

lightly
my fingers danced over
your hands
engulfing mine
warmly, heavily
so much
larger than my own
which seem
childlike

YEN

the daily haze of
what needs to be done
obfuscates the
inner carbon, the
unformed diamond,
the great dreams

ground down, barely
nubs of what they
once were
settling, accepting
contentment

instead of still
grasping
for unmitigated
joy

embodied Tantalus,
unable to drink from
the cup of desire
or eat the fruition of
the heart's wish

incapable of breaking
free of the shackles
of necessity and tedium

and dreaming of flying,
soaring into the sun
(though perhaps not
as high as Icarus)

UNTITLED

impossible to change
at my very core
i'm your heart's desire
you can't see that about me
blinded, as you are, by
the facade, the cover
leaving me
confused, lost
longing to hear the words
that will never be applied
never be uttered
(at least not to me)
alone i stay, quiet
empty
waiting for the one who will
change it all

UNTITLED

teach me love
let me fall under
your spell
- just for a moment -
let me learn what it
feels like to
be held

teach me patience
let me wait through
your confusion
- 'til understanding comes -
let me learn what it
feels like to
trust completely

teach me strength
let me stand for more
than myself
- side by side -
let me learn what it
feels like to
be part of
another

teach me love

don't leave me

alone

LOVE'S INSOMNIAC

who needs insomnia
for the sake of not sleeping

give me insomnia
in a night of whispered promises
in a twilight of kisses
and gentle caresses

let me leave behind
long nights of vision slightly
blurred by staring at the clock

let me forget
senses dulled and actions slowed
due to the incomprehensible
exhaustion

let me fall asleep,
not cold and lonely in
the early hours of sunrise
but held in the embrace
of love

UNTITLED

i dream of fantasy
the universe brings us together
we swim in passion and love

awakening in the cool, sharp reality
i mourn that which i'll never have
cursing the fantasy, the dream

the manifestation of what i want
the only way i'll ever have it
bitter, spiteful I rage against it
longing for it and hating it
all at once

i dream of fantasy
of you and me
and of love

FAIRY TALE PRINCESS

as a little girl
hair in pigtails, knees scraped from yet
another fall learning to ride a bike
i dreamt of a white knight, in armor
gleaming and bright,
his shield brilliant and sword sharp, glinting in the noonday sun

he was the stuff of legends, of
fairytales
rescuing the princess (me, of course) from
despair and bleakness
riding into twilight, falling in love

as a young woman
i see my knight -
armor dull and chipped, the shine worn down
sword sharp, but barely -
only really useful in self-defense -
less rescuing me, more that we save one another

- for a little while, at least -

the little girl inside still yearns,
still dreams, hopeful
but not me

FAIRYTALES

glistening
cubic zirconia
the airbrushed
ideal

delusions of
a life
unattainable
fraudulent

heartache
wrapped in silken
half truths and
velvet deceit

well spun bedtime
stories misleading
generations between
charybdis and scylla

tripping, drunk on becoming
cinderella, beauty, snow white
we forget to become
who we are

how cruel is fate to
guide a life's destiny based
on the picking of a flower
or a forgotten invitation?
what lessons do children learn
from fairy tales of steps that
are a thousand knife wounds
and a poisoned apple?
what does a child walk away with
after reading such tales?
the dragon can be killed?
the witch outsmarted?
that love conquers all? - now that,
a dangerous illusion to
teach in a world so
dangerous and wild

WRETCHED

dark, twisted, cold
how alone in your world
you must feel

choking on bitterness
jealousy crowding your throat
cloying and stifling

difficult to breathe

i stare, awestruck, at how
prettily you decorate your world
- pink fluff and glittering tiaras,
midwestern royalty in
commoner's clothing -

all to hide the putrescence
of your life
in its garish, lurid colors
and blinding metallics
fading under a hot, scorching sun

i cannot fathom the loneliness
you must daily endure

from driving away the very people
you once claimed as friends, as family,
because you were too busy

admiring yourself in the
funhouse mirror
of your self-perception

INFLAMMATION

like an itch
just under the skin
irritated, red

your brazen disregard
for personal responsibility
and blatant distaste for
doing even the most basic
of tasks

scratches, bites
at my skin like
sand whipping across
the desert

i must admit my
bafflement at your
attitude

why are you even here?

UNTITLED

can you even see it?
   the hypocrisy in all this?
are you aware, at all,
   how ridiculous you sound?
a choice is before you:
   change or don't;
   act or don't.
but you need to open your eyes
   and be honest with yourself
in order to see that choice.
what you say, how you behave
   when they don't match
   when the incongruence hurts you
you only have yourself to blame

wake the fuck up
grow the fuck up
be an adult already

POT, MEET KETTLE

(hello pot, meet kettle.)
fascinating.
astonishing, really,
that you can't see how your
   very complaint
is so very applicable to you.
frustrating
to see you sit there with this litany
   of how you've been wronged
and know that you can't (or won't)
   own your part in this mess.
how can you sit and expect change
   if you aren't willing to make personal change?
how can you demand a fair shake
   when history has shown that you avoid the same?
i hope you're ready to swallow the status quo
because that's all that you're perpetuating

BITTERNESS

you sit across from me
living in your pretty little world
where everyone is like you

fuck you
and your bullshit

i have held you when you cried
i have defended you from your fears
i have lifted you back onto your feet

fuck you
and your bullshit

you spin sparkling little myths and
make believe, what you think
the world is like

you never really did see

fuck you
i will not be cast aside
i will not be treated like this

whoever you are - for i do not know you

prepare yourself for the worst

i'm just getting started

UNTITLED

withholding
moments of
anger
and betrayal

biting lips
and tongue
till chapped and
raw

not wanting
to risk
loss
pain
drama

choking on
the rage
simmering
below the surface

until it
poisons a
quiet place
inside

UNTITLED

battle lines
drawn in
anger, frustration,
bitterness
gripping tightly
(hard to breathe)

forced to let go
relax, forget
forgive

but memory is long

and slippery

so forward in a
mixed media and
whirlwind of
emotions

so predictable, right?
my path well-trod,
no deviations.
except…
there are these footprints
meandering in a whole 'nother direction
no one sees them but me.
like i'm two people, one real,
the other ephemeral
but all the same individual
conflicting and cooperating

you think you know me so well…
predictable, right?

we'll see.

UNTITLED

at the edge
– ground crumbling
beneath my feet –
staring down
the long drop
knowing just how close
to grasping for purchase
i am

decide

step back, regroup
  recharge

    or

fall apart

some choice. no choice.

UNTITLED

raw -
a jagged wound -
that salt is rubbed in
(burning pain, sharp and brilliant)
the friction wearing down,
breaking down,
until nothing is left
just finding a way
   to hunker down
   duck below
   go unnoticed
until you can break free
(if only for a while)
and breathe
and heal

UNTITLED

twists and
pitfalls
plague the disjointed
interpersonal
moments between us
slivers of truth
interspersed
with lies
- fall like rain
from your lips -

how do we
go forward?

what reparations could
bring us
back to harmony?

there is no map
no clues
to find the even path

UNTITLED

a flicker
a passing shadow of
what could have been
gone
between breaths
before it ever could be
known and
accepted
now, grappling
with both the
learning
and the
losing
all at once

UNTITLED

two halves
so very different
but fit together
so flawlessly
smoothly
amazed,
so enamored
with complete opposites
within a whole
how to reconcile
such disparities
the paradoxical
you

quiet
the soft thrum of the heat
the tick of the clock
the only sounds to disrupt the night

reflection
circling thoughts
fleeting bits of memory
passing desires
all drifting in my mind

time
trudging along now
weary and stubborn
wishing that it would just
hurry along

EXHAUSTION

weight
dragging me down
pace slowing and
lashes brushing
together

a bone-deep
weariness
not easily escaped

the comfort of the
dreamless sleep
(much desired, a
mirage on the horizon)
out of arm's reach

hours still to go
- as the morning glint
of the sun's rays
overtake the world -

before climbing
into
bed

and drifting

away

INSOMNIAC

blearily i stare
at the vivid red
numbers

that never change

willing time
to move ahead
at more than a
snail's pace

in the dark
i lie, awake
and alert

sleep is
ephemeral
constantly just
beyond my fingertips

frustrated
i fling the covers
away and
roll out of bed
annoyed

resigning myself
to another night
of working

NIGHTMARE

it was the fragment of the dream, really,
that left me shaking awake, trembling,
throat raw and pained from hours of the
silent scream i never released
shivering, cold and hollow, i wiped
the sweat of horror from my brow and
traced the sorrow along my cheeks
trying to banish the dark
in the twilight of the morning
curling deep into the covers
reticently i return to sleep
in hopes of lighter - or no - dreams
in the hours before dawn

UNTITLED

stars glitter sharply in the
crisp cold of midnight
the edge of a winter that has not yet come
standing outside shivering
a choice between illusion and truth
air dances around you
warm and tantalizing
an oasis on the horizon
always out of reach
others have found their place
by a fire, inside wrapped in
thick blankets, drinking in
the liquid velvet of chocolate
still i stand outside
skin bare to the cold air
waiting alone

UNTITLED

dancing under the stars,
the night clear and bright -
cool, too, so the flames,
licking the air, warm
the soul
dancing the stories of
the ancestors, of our families
dancing the gifts which
they gave to us
dancing in every moment,
waking and slumbering,
the very power of life

MOONLIGHT

in the dark of the night
the world pale in starlight
the soul quiets
listening to the thrum of
earth and sky

reaching out towards
the growing light of dawn
tentative and soft
the soul stills
feeling the peace in
the fragile rays

night shifts to day
the ageless transition of hues
the soul stretches
seeking its limits, its boundaries,
its safe haven within time

WINTER'S KISS

shivering,
the gust slicing
against me,
i walk

into the first
breath
of Winter's Kiss

crisp browns, reds, oranges
crunching -
my steps quick
and brisk -

reveling in
the darkening season
the long night

before the return
of light

i hear the
whirring
of the air conditioner
how it hums
and breathes cool
air
into the room

i hear the footfalls of
cats
prowling their space
sacred
to them - and others -

i hear my
own
heartbeat and
soft breaths

in the solitude
of a quiet summer's day

while sitting
- peaceful -
- comfortable -
in my favorite store

TOTWC

The roots of our tradition,
while still young,
reach deep.
They stretch into the
ground, shaking through
the soil,
touching the Mother.

Once a tiny sapling,
it now reaches skyward -
a tree young, but strong.
It's leaves dancing in
the wind,
touching the Father.

We have all been the branches,
stretching outward into the world,
having grown from our
foundation, our trunk -
you.

We've become the seeds
of our own trees,
ready to begin
our journey.

As we fall free,
Reborn,
we carry the traditions
forward -
making the world a
better place
one witch
at a
time.

BREAK

murmurs of
layers of conversations
as people absorb
the beginning half
of class
they stretch legs, bodies,
minds
a few dart out to smoke
before finding their
seats again
to listen in rapt attention

a model for
the rest of us.

walked a long, rough road
– pushed yourself here –
to build such an incredible place
for others to learn and grow.
a soul scarred by history
but beautiful in its strength.
a face of the Divine
just beneath the surface.
a leader in magick and in hope.

but mostly just
my friend.

INCENSE

a cool autumn
afternoon

inhaling the
fragrances of
calendula
lavender
cedar or
myrrh

blending of
scents
petals
stems
leaves

to prepare
a special
blend

for
Mabon

pools of
lilac
cornflower
teal
rouge
across the cold
surface

cylinder of
cooling wax
brimming with
potential,
possibility

a history of
rainbows
dapple the
workbench

where
magick begins

there is a point
in the midst of ritual
when time stops.
the circle has been cast,
the elements called.
candles have been lit
and the Lord and Lady invited.
that timeless moment –
  it fills you with a
  Divine warmth.
it's that moment when you
understand what it means
that the Divine is within you
that the Lord and Lady live in your
  heart and soul
that you are never without them,
  never alone
you are Divine and the Divine is you

i approach her in a moonlit field
surrounded by dancing wolves and prancing deer
faeries weaving in flowers sleeping
trees swaying to the music of the wind.
"for all you've done enough i cannot thank,
love and guidance there to ask,
what more can i do for thee,
my life is in your grasp."
Mother, Giver,
Lover, Killer,
reaches out to me
"my child, my jewel, my creation and love,
my wish is this and naught else:
live in the light of the celestial guides,
bathe in the love of life,
dance in the mists' magickal lore,
sow the seeds for future souls.
become teacher, student, leader, follower;
remember your oath to me -
share the truth of the lore of old
and in rites hold me dear."
by light of moon and dark of night
the truth of sacred rites
of worship and reverence
filled me to the brim -
cup overflowing with truth and love
sword held high in awe.
circle glowing white hot bright
warmth envelops me.
awaking in the morning light
in a grove of oaks,
the only hint of things that night
was trampled grass around me.

what truly transpired that sacred night
my mind will never know -
my spirit lost to the eternal moonlight
of her strength and love,
truth lies in the dew-stained grass
and the circle drawn nigh.

i love the light within
that shimmers just 'neath the skin
the little piece of divinity inside us
whose glow brings people together
i love that gentle reminder
that the Creator is walking this world
inside my sisters and brothers
(the ones i like and the others, too)
it's the opportunity to move forward
in an interpersonal way
and honor the Divine within me,
relearning to love my being

CPSIA information can be obtained
at www.ICGtesting.com
Printed in the USA
BVHW04*2242310518
517859BV00002B/3/P